Moonbeams

and

Scattered Thoughts

Traveling Through the Dark to Find My Light

By

Celeste J. Holloway

Healing is not a straight line, it's a labyrinth to the places in my mind. In order to free your mind, you must unlock those doors

Celeste J. Holloway

This life will walk down paths of roses and through roads paved with fire while you're drenched in gasoline…you have to prepare yourself for both. Hearts break and minds become clouded, unable to differentiate between reality and illusion, your decision to move forward will make or break you. Piecing yourself back together takes courage, strength and willpower to see it through to the sanity you seek. This is a piece of my journey to wholeness. The aftermath…

Celeste J. Holloway

Contents

Dedicated to my babies,
thank you for inspiring me
to be better, I love you My
3 J's!
To my family and friends,
who've become family,
thank you all for listening
& offering a helping hand
in any way, I love y'all!

Celeste J Holloway

Every Second Every Minute

Alone with my thoughts, thinking about my

life and all

Each time it was bad, I've always gotten up

after the fall

Perfect? Not even remotely close

But I have more to be thankful for than most

Lost my dad at a young age, he almost killed

my mama too

Been lied to, cheated on, after saying I Do

Became a single mother, not once but times

three

Tell me once more how hard times can be??

I've been through the most, couldn't walk

but I was able to crawl

Every second, every minute, I'm grateful I'm

able to ball

Living life to fullest, with my family right by

my side

If no one else is there for me, my team is

always down to ride...

Be grateful for where you are because it

ain't where
you were, you're making progress

The Journey Back to Self

Found

Face to face with the scars & pain that I've blocked out for

years

Words fill my mind, never to escape my lips.. feelings, here

come the tears

Wounds open, heart jumps from my body to lie on the

floor

Everything that was packed away, never to be seen again

has bursted through the door

No more locks. Bare. Soul exposed. Naked. Unable to

hide

Healing is not the same as hiding behind my pride

Cleaning out this emotional baggage, for good this go
round

Tension my body usually holds is subsiding, heading
for peace...glad the hidden compartment has been
found

Healing

My energy flows differently as I'm working

through this process

Small changes, winning small battles, slowly

seeing progress

Bridges burned, from my notebook pages are

torn

In my current state, my niceness has been worn

No longer trying to satisfy

Those that only sell me lies

You're here because you wanted something

from me

Not because you love & support my dreams, so
I'll just be

Off to the left

Praying. Helping the Lord heal myself

Memories faded

Time that's been wasted

None of those will ever change

But the way I deal with others & my

thought patterns

I've had to rearrange

Should've caught me when I was still

stuck

On pleasing others & making them
happy, cause now you're out of luck...

You Lied

Drained me of all my pride

I was so proud to be yours, would've followed you

to
the end of the world

Just because you were all mine and I was your girl

Turns out, you belonged to all of them as well

Not once, more than twice...honestly I can't truly

tell

The number of times you stepped out of our life

For god's sake, I'm your wife

Special, unique, different from any other

In a way that excites you, not like your mother

Your rib, your side, if your cup was bare, I'd gladly
share mine

Now I'm drowning in sorrow, pass me the wine

Don't need a glass, give me the bottle

Tiptoeing around ain't getting it, diving in full

throttle

I gave you parts of me unknown to another
man
It didn't mean a thing, or was this your plan?
To take me out so far, I have no chance of
coming back
Being the yin to my yang, all that I lack
Only to push me back
Out all alone, I want to attack
Your girlfriend, that whore
But hurting you is what I desire more...

My Pen is Therapy

If I can't open my heart to my mama or my

friend

That only leaves my pen filled with ink on which

I can depend

My pains, the pleasures

From my lowest point to when I've come into
my treasure

I shall bare my soul, everything visible to the

naked eye

Down to the crevices buried beneath my heart,

that only tumble out when I cry

To release the anger and the pain

Is to retrain the energy, from depletion to gain

Using the pain to grow like I hadn't done before

I sit down, organize my thoughts
and write once more....

Deep

The smile

My beauty

I have a keen sense of fashion

I keep my hair & nails done

I go to parties

I have friends

I have fun...so why am I sad?

Why am I angry?

Why do I feel I am unworthy of life?

Each day I wake up, I don't understand why I

feel this
way.

It hurts

The pain runs deep

No one understands

The exterior & the interior do not match

My smile is a facade, meant to keep me
going from day to day

I cannot live this way...

I want help but I can't explain what's
wrong...

Darkness

Some nights were so dark, the light of day
couldn't seep through

Bitterness, hatred & anger are all I would spew

From my mind, from my mouth...the heart
encased in my body was as icy as a Polar Bear

My body language spoke the truth my smile

tried to
hide, a reality seen in all my appearance, down
to my
hair

No stylist, only my satin scarf & my pillows
filled my
days and my nights

I couldn't quite put my finger on it, but

something
wasn't right...

Luv vs Love

I text I love you

You reply luv u

I say I miss you

You reply miss u

So, tell me what's missing?

You are!

It's not genuine

It's not inclusive of you

It is merely a reply to say I want to keep

You around until I say I've had enough

Moving forward. You say luv u

I say Thank You! What's missing?

Me!

Now, I simply reply

Giving you the same energy, less effort

Your Way

Sitting in the darkness, vision as clear as a
sunny day
Reminiscing on all the times I let you have
your way
There was no connection, yet I let you in
my sphere
Now I'm avoiding you & we're here
No conversations, blocked you on social
media and my line
Stop asking about me when you see my
fam, I'mma always be fine
A want is all you were, nowhere near a
necessity to me
When you walked through the door, I
already had all my own..now you can be
free
To run with them hoes and let them use
you up like a sugar daddy Just remember
you had an intellectual that wanted to help
you grow, way more than just a
baddie...Irreplaceable

Giving Back

The back & forth is constant, like an ongoing

custody battle

I'll save you the trouble, bow out gracefully...so
silence the chatter
My soul is void, empty, when you're part of the
conversation
I do not hate you, I've healed..become love, locked

out
negativity with meditation
Your words no longer have any affect in my life

So my gift to you, all the lies about taking me as
your wife

I give the lies back to you, hoping they keep you

warm at night

Memories, chances with you have all vanished, the
normalcy has returned, getting myself right

Calling Back my Energy

My energy flows in a new direction

I understand the importance of love and affection

Not to outside sources, but to the brown eyes I stare
into day after day
When I look in the mirror thanking God for making a

way

This beautiful mind

That chooses to be kind

The tired eyes that see through the BS & the lies

These same eyes provide an outlet for my cries

During times when I couldn't give or receive love

But now I am capable of both, putting my needs
above

Any other in my life

Without self love, I was existing, not
living my life

Illusions of my Perception

I create these visions within my mind

Involving other people, making reality hard to find

A love affair with hopes & dreams

A relationship with plots & schemes

The people before me are sent to me, I'm a job for
them to complete

No family, no friends, another entity with whom

they'll compete

For a shot at making their dreams a reality, but I'm

not in their race

I'm sitting here, alone, moving at my own pace

Love doesn't live here, it's a door I have yet to open

Pain, anger & sadness fill my brain...but I'm hoping

To reach inner peace, a destination
I'm working so hard to find

Patience, forgiveness & self

reflection tell me I'm
heading there, in due time

Your Side

Empty promises

Words without effort or intent

No veil covering my eyes

No excuses to protect me from your lies

I see the true meaning of who you are

One sided

All about self gain

My journey was the ride I needed

To get away from you

Selfish

Greedy

Saying anything to bait me

Pacify my insecurities

No longer

Me vs Me

When I needed you to protect me, you

weren't there When I wanted you to speak

up, you were mute

When I didn't know what love was, you had

no
answers

Filled with rage, holding in the pain

Self destruction was a winding road that
went on for miles without a beautiful view

Black days, red nights

Intoxicated to numb the feelings

No way out

I needed you, I needed you, I needed you

I yelled into the mirror at my reflection

She gave her tears, my red eyes spilled out
sorrow and apology at all once

I will forever be there for you. I accept you,

flaws and all. I FINALLY LOVE YOU

My Voice

The path I desire to take is clearly painted on the
forefront of my mind

When I open my eyes, I see smoke...my visibility is

significantly decreased

Vision. Hard work, desire are all part of my

strategy

Yet everything remains so unclear

I paint the pictures

I say the prayer

I have faith, I see it before it's there

I move with the weight of the world on my
shoulder

Working on removing barriers from my mind

On day at a time

My sight clears

My drive increases

I hear my own words..

My Reflection of a Stranger

I'M LOOKING IN THE MIRROR BUT THE REFLECTION

DOES NOT LOOK FAMILIAR TO ME

COLD, BLACK EYES WITH SCARS EQUALLY AS DARK ARE

ALL I SEE

A STRANGER. A FACE I LONG TO REMEMBER, WELCOME

BACK TO A SANE PLACE

LORD PROTECT ME AS I WALK THROUGH THE VALLEY

OF DEATH, PROVIDE ME WITH GRACE

DEPRESSION IS A DARK CAVE IN WHICH YOUR

HAPPINESS IS HELD PRISONER & CAN'T COME OUT

A STOP, NOT A DESTINATION, ON YOUR HEALING

ROUTE

YET, SOME NEVER MAKE IT THROUGH

HOW CAN I BE SO SURE I'M COMING OUT TOO?

Mine

All these voices, all these faces

Various types of energy and vibrations

Centering myself, turn my vibe down low

Build up my tolerance, watch my

resistance grow

My inner peace will radiate from within,

Gone is my foolish pride

Cleansing my aura, my mind & everything

inside

Beauty is only skin deep, It tends to fade
away

But this inner peace is everlasting, I know

it's here to stay

Flow

The toxicity leaked from her core

Like the monthly release of vital fluids

She felt drained

Yet, renewed at the same time

Her perspective changed

Life became brighter

She welcomed the new life

brewing Inside her

Thought pattern upcycled

Negative thoughts no longer wore the blue

ribbon Appreciation for herself and the

second chance she'd
been given

Life 2.0

Changing old habits by reprogramming

my mind

The thoughts, like my voice, have always

been there;

yet, were hard to find

Escaping my comfort zone to reach new

heights

Walking out of the shadows, into the
limelight

Life has so much more to offer, why

hadn't I stepped

out before?

I guess I wasn't ready, now it's time to

explore

Owning My Life

I hurt for a long time

It was everyone else's fault

I was angry

I was discouraged

I was sad

I was depressed

I was bitter

I was in pain

My words were harsh

My soul was dark

My heart was closed

My eyes were black

I couldn't see that the problem was ME

After playing games with someone's heart

I said Lord, I'm tired...I don't recognize this
person I've become

The tears poured

I opened up the closet in my mind

Unpacked all the baggage from years ago

Felt the pain, dealt with the insecurities, cried
the tears I held back for so many years

I acknowledged my faults, took responsibility

for my
wrongdoings, started my healing process
I prayed, went into a period of self reflection,

isolated
myself from my distractions
I rebuilt myself

Daily mantras, prayer, meditation, isolation,
learned to love me for who I am and the
person I'm becoming... I'm on my way

What it could've been

No matter how fast I run, I can't escape my

broken
heart
The tears fall like rain during a hurricane

My heart beats slowly, as it yearns to become
whole once more

Emotions rage. Anger. Frustration. Shame.

Fear. Lust. Depression.

I'm drowning in what should've been, could've

been

So much so I can't see the possibilities of
today, let alone tomorrow

My tears are freeing, necessary for me to get

out of my own head

Held On

Tight grip, looks forward to hearing your voice

Time goes on, calling & texting you is now an

option, not a choice

My grip has been released, I see you the way

you see me

As something to do during bored times or be

seen as infrequent as I want to be

I used to see us so vividly, now you aggravate

my soul, no longer care

It built up from times when you left me there

While you played with this one & that one &
God knows who else was part of your mix

We're completely broken, impossible to fix

The tears fall as I release you from my mind

Don't worry, I have come to terms with leaving

you behind....

Deal with it

Reminiscing as the rage comes roaring like a
lion
Bittersweet moments
Thankful for the closure, bitter about the
occurrence Feeling those emotions I
suppressed for such a long time
Releasing the pain is not as poetic as I'd hoped
Tears. Pain. Anger.
My once hollow insides are now open to
receive love
I am worthy
I believe I can give love

Saving Her

In the midst of the chaos and loud screams

Her attention was drawn back to her goals, her

dreams

The outside noise pierced her windows, she

knew she had to fight

To maintain her energy, balance her darkness

with more light

At the end of the day, she only heard her own

voice in her head

She is in tune with her own energy, keeping her

spirit fed

Come out and play

Looking into the mirror

Past the metaphorical mask I wear each day to face

the world

I see the scars & pain, the parts of myself I

considered ugly

Instead of shying away from them, I welcome them

to come out of hiding, breathe for a change I sit with

them

Feel them

Uncover them, searching for the root of their causes

One by one, I integrate those shadows into my daily

life

They belong,
the pain that accompanied them for so
many year no long exists
because I understand the cause

I am not ashamed

I am not guilty

I survived!!

I battled the demons

I've made peace with my past

Work in Progress

I'm no satin, far from silk...more like wool,

still being polished

The girl I was 12 years ago has been

completely demolished

She has been rebuilt from the ground
Up to her head, where she's now crowned
Perfect, nah... that's so overrated
Refer back to what I'd previously stated
Still a work in progress, a lil rough around the

edges

Still sensitive, beautiful like a diamond that
precious
Worth more alone than she'd ever be with

another

Graduated from princess up to Queen
Mother....

Me & You

I won't hate me because of the pain that you hide

I won't hate me because you can't love me due to your pride

I won't hate me because you don't understand who I am right now

I won't hate me because anger in your head is all you allow

I don't conform to your standards in any way, shape, fashion or form

So you have a reason to hate me, I'm far from the norm...

Internal Wounds & External Bandages

Changing your physical does nothing to

restructure the inside

You can lose weight, grow your hair..but

that won't kill your pride

You character flaws can be hid like a clam

birthing a pearl

Eventually, your true self will begin to unfurl

For all in the world to see the ugliness inside

You can run from your truth for a while, but

you can't continue to hide...

Changing

Some come for whole seasons

Others come for specific reasons

People enter into our lives to teach

Each one you meet is not made to reach

That special place in your heart that

earns them a title

Family or friend, they're replaceable, not
vital

Good, bad, indifferent, they aren't all the

same

But in the end, we're usually glad they
came...

Learn to release, when it's time

Moving forward is normal, not a crime

Let Go

I've heard the saying if you love something, let it go

If it comes back, it's yours—if it doesn't, you'll never know

Heard another saying that explains people leave & come back to finish what they started
Which could be tearing you apart, ain't that cold hearted?
I say it's heart over mind

Remove the emotions, press rewind

Was your time together fun and uplifting, did your heart skip a beat when they came around?
Or was is detrimental to your growth, so much so

their voice became just a sound?

Weigh your options, remember people can and do change
If you feel bad vibes, move around and leave them estranged

Time Wasted

All those years

Fussing, fighting, flowing tears

Memories of us are not that great

I catch you doing wrong, you lie and I take the

bait Because we have history, once loved one

another, held one another through the night

As daylight broke, this female and that female

wants to fight

Me... for a man with whom I lost energy, wasted

effort and gave too much time

Finally, I can say if loving you was a crime

I'd be set free

To live the life I deserve, my head and heart

both agree....

Reality Check

Smiles in your face, hates behind your back even
harder

The disdain mounts as you progress and become

smarter

How did you get here? Cause with them, you haven't

changed

Your time became limited as your priorities were

rearranged

Do better, make life easier became my motto

Apparently to those that we're once on your team,
that was a hard pill to swallow

You've supported their dreams, each and every one

Now that it's my turn, the seam that held the bond
tight has become undone...

Careful who you call your family, lover or a friend

Find you when it's beneficial to their plan, no regard
for yours, how well do people pretend

Under the Influence

Under the influence of depression, my mind said this
is good! My heart said no

Unsure of the route I should take, the words flowed

naturally

My actions aligned with my words, my insides knew

you'd be a casualty

Unable to utter the words, I took part in the charade

Bored out of my mind, antsy, swimming out of
depression...happy, yet ashamed

You became collateral damage as I set upon my
journey to healing
Your voice, your face and your energy all became

unappealing

You aligned with my darkness, undeserving of my

light

I apologize for taking hold of your
attention with no future in sight....

I evaluate myself often, to see where I'm slacking & where I can improve. My self evaluation also examines the company I keep. As I've grown, I've lost friends and family because we don't have the same paths. Negative mindsets will push people away from you. Negativity is draining, to say the least. If I'm distant now, know there's a reason for it. I need not explain, nor do I care to discuss the situation. I wish you the best and I pray you
WIN in all your endeavors!